The Waterfall Effect

Six Principles
for
Productive Leadership

Paul H. Burton

The Waterfall Effect
Six Principles for Productive Leadership

Copyright © 2012 by Paul H. Burton

Published by:
Paul H. Burton
www.quietspacing.com

Cover design and interior layout: www.TheBookProducer.com

Printed in the United States of America

ISBN 978-0-9818911-4-9

DEDICATION

To all those who understand that leadership is
fundamentally about achieving results.

About Paul H. Burton

Paul H. Burton is a former attorney, software executive, and successful entrepreneur. He helps clients regain command of their day, get more done, and enjoy greater personal and professional satisfaction. Paul is available for keynote presentations, interactive training seminars, and individualized coaching services.

You can learn more about Paul and his work at
www.quietspacing.com.

CONTENTS

CHAPTER 1

The Most Important Thing

Some say people are an organization's most valuable asset. Others say it's the customers. Still, others say it's the organization's reputation—its brand—that is most important. They're all wrong.

It's time. Time is every organization's most valuable asset. It's also the most valuable asset to the people who make up the organization, for it is within the construct of time that everything else occurs.

Before reaching for our swords or donning our breastplates, let's clarify. That time is every organization's most important asset isn't a challenge to the physics or metaphysics of existence. Others have made much more learned and well-reasoned arguments on this subject, such as Stephen Hawking in *A Brief History of Time* and Alan Lightman in *Einstein's Dreams*.

Time's place at the top of the list here simply aligns our thinking to recognize how much we use and rely on it within our organizations. In fact, many of the measurements organizations use to determine progress and success inherently include time.

We've all heard that "time is money"! It's true. Here are some examples:

- If we can **shorten** the sales cycle, it will take **less time** to get **more** customers.

- If we can **reduce** absenteeism, **more** of our people will spend **more time** at work.

- If we can **shorten** individual development time, our people will learn **more** skills in **less time**.

- If we can **reduce** interruptions and distractions, we will spend **more time** focused on getting things done.

We use time-based metrics in making many of our personal and professional decisions.

Whose Time Is Most Important?

If time is an organization's most valuable asset, the next logical question is, whose time within the organization is the most valuable? Is it that of the stakeholders—shareholders and/or owners—who invested their money and hard work? What about that of the line staff, the people who get it done every day? Maybe it's that of management, since one manager can oversee the productivity of many people. It's got to be that of executive management, those responsible for steering the ship toward its objectives, right?

No. The most important time within the organization is your time. Yes, yours. And before reaching for the sword and breastplate again, understand that the reason for this is the **Waterfall Effect**.

The Waterfall Effect: A Cascading of Benefits

All organizations are made up of people. In fact, if people did not show up at their jobs every day, there wouldn't be an organization. Therefore, the time each person gives to the organization is vitally important to the organization's very existence.

That time can be used well or squandered. Squandered time is a true waste—once spent, time is lost forever. There's no rewind, and there are no do-overs.

That's where the Waterfall Effect comes in. If the time an organization has available to it is used by the right people who are focused on the right objectives and are working with the right resources, the benefits of that use cascade down through the organization and out to the clients and customers. Simply stated, using time well creates a waterfall of good results.

EXAMPLE: THE SALES PITCH

One great example of the Waterfall Effect is Outdoorplay, Inc. Outdoorplay is an online retailer of outdoor recreational gear. Since 1998, the founders have enjoyed developing it into a healthy, growing business. In fact, in 2006, they groomed a management team to run the day-to-day operations.

Focusing the management team on the right activities, people, and objectives has allowed the founders to pursue other interests. One started a new business. The other went surfing in Peru. This is an example of what the Waterfall Effect meant for the two owners of the company.

Here's an extension of the same example. Because they have a great team of people who attend to Outdoorplay's day-to-day needs, the founders can focus on a very important business metric—the conversion rate. The conversion rate is the number of visitors to a website who "convert" into customers—those who find the products and information they need to make an informed buying decision and are then able to make their purchases and check out without incident.

There are several benefits to increasing the conversion rate:

- Higher sales figures: Outdoorplay sells more products.

- Lower toll-free bill: People don't require as much live assistance via the toll-free phone number.

- Few call center staff: Fewer calls require fewer people to staff the phones.

- More-engaged employees: People can focus their effort on more interesting work when they aren't answering the same questions over and over.

- Happy customers: Anyone who shops on-line knows that we have a great buying experience when we find what we want and can check out quickly and easily.

As the above example illustrates, a host of benefits cascade down through the organization and out to the customers/clients whenever the Waterfall Effect occurs. To make the point even clearer, here is a list of the benefits:

- **Better Customer Satisfaction.** Whenever we meet or exceed customer/client expectations, the organization benefits.

- **Better Employee/Customer Retention.** Whenever our employees are more engaged in their jobs and our customers/clients are more satisfied with our performance, the retention rates for both groups are higher.

- **Better Reputation.** If we are producing a large number of benefits for a large number of people inside and outside the organization, our reputations are enhanced.

- **Better Success.** Success is a feeling for people—we feel successful, accomplished, in charge—and a result for organizations using self-defined metrics. The greatest benefit of the Waterfall Effect is that it produces success for both the organization and the people who breathe life into it.

So how do we produce the Waterfall Effect again and again? The detailed answer to that question is contained below. But before jumping into those details, one final opening point must be made.

It's about People!

So often, leadership discussions presume the type of formal leadership generally associated with titles, promotions, or election results. Specifically, leadership is couched in terms of who's in charge.

This book takes a more general approach to leadership—that is, leadership is about what people do versus what they say or what their titles proclaim them to be. In essence, everyone can be a leader. As such, everyone can produce the Waterfall Effect.

The Six Principles

In the next few chapters, we will be digging down into the six principles that take "leaders" to produce the Waterfall Effect. The true purpose of these six principles is for people to use them to become productive leaders—people who get things done in a manner that generates the greatest organizational and individual success possible:

- **Developing Field Vision**—the need to assimilate and respond to dynamic environments

- **Keeping the Glass Half-Full**—the impact of attitude on group psyche

- **Leveraging the Value of Silence**—the benefits of being quiet

- **Peeling Back the Onion**—the reward of uncovering the hidden potential in others

- **Setting the Bar**—the importance of establishing and maintaining expectations

- **Triaging Priorities**—the reality of constant appraisal of what needs doing "now"

Improving our ability to produce any of these principles makes us better leaders. Any combination of them increases the likelihood of creating the Waterfall Effect.

Exercise: Describe a Waterfall Effect

Please take a moment to think about the last time you were a participant in or a witness to a Waterfall Effect. Use the space below to jot down a description of the event(s) and the benefits received by those involved and those to whom the benefits accrued.

_____

_____

_____

_____

_____

CHAPTER 2

Developing Field Vision
The Need to Assimilate and Respond to Dynamic Environments

Leadership discussions invariably fall prey to sports analogies. For better or worse, the same holds true here.

The concept of "Developing Field Vision" arose from describing football quarterbacks and their ability to quickly assess the dynamic activity midplay and react accordingly. It seems fair then that we allow the sports analogy to take flight in this chapter.

An NFL quarterback has memorized approximately 250 plays. During the game, he is responsible for coordinating ten other players on his team while paying attention to the eleven players on the defense who are constantly shifting their positions not so conveniently. While all this is going on, our leader must decide whether to audibly change the play. And he must do it inside the thirty-second play clock.

Once the ball is snapped, the quarterback must begin another dynamic assessment involving all the moving players, half of whom are trying to help him and half of whom are trying to tackle him. If the play is a running play, the quarterback's only job is to get the ball to the running back. If it's a pass play, the quarterback must decipher the coverage and the protection, determine which receiver is the most open, and throw the ball to that player.

The endgame for the quarterback is to score enough points so that his team wins the game. The speed and fluidity of our leader's actions are no accident. He has studied and practiced the plays, defenses, and alternative courses of action again and again throughout the year. Over time, successful quarterbacks are described as having great field vision—the ability to see the entire playing field as it unfolds and thus react accordingly.

Visualize the Path

So what are some of the basic tenets of developing this field vision? What can we learn from our quarterback that will give us a leg up in our own dynamic working environment?

The first lesson we can learn is to *visualize the path*. We all know that most successful endeavors involve completing a series of steps to reach the goal. The same is true for football. Rarely does one big play result in a touchdown. Usually, it takes numerous smaller plays to score points. The play selection is never random. In fact, it is highly dependent on the specific situation at hand, but the objective of all the plays is to carve a path toward the end zone.

Achieving productive leadership—getting things accomplished—mandates that the leader visualize the path to success. Stated most succinctly by the Cheshire cat in *Alice in Wonderland* (the movie), if we don't know our destination, "then any path will do."

To achieve a specific result, or to move an entire team of people toward the same destination, a leader must give serious and repeated consideration to the path used to get there. Consequently, visualizing the path is as dynamic as the surroundings along the path being taken. Things change throughout the time it takes to move along. This makes the monitoring function almost as important as the original route selection.

STORY: THE PROP GUY

Joe Clarke, the self-proclaimed "prop guy" for the Wynn Las Vegas stage show *Le Rêve*, recently spoke about the intersection of creativity and productivity. His talk was as fascinating as it was incisive. The question presented was, how do we create this fabulous multifaceted stage show from the ideas that form in our head?

During one segment of his talk, Joe paused, looked around the room, and then addressed the audience again. "You look around this room and see a conference hall set up for a speaker. I look around this room and see four blank walls and a cement floor. From there, I make a list of everything I'll need to create a conference room setup for a speaker. Next, I walk through my warehouse and gather the carpet for the floor, the fabric for the walls, the lights to hang from the ceiling, and so on. The final task of assembly produces the result we are experiencing today, but it is the effort of visualizing the end result that makes it possible to produce it."

What a fine description of visualizing the path! Joe broke down the objective—creating a meeting room—into very definable subparts—steps, if you will. He then gathered the materials needed to achieve the result. The final effort of assembling the various items produced the room that previously existed only as an idea.

Working to produce organizational results is a similar process. It's an option to throw a Hail Mary and hope your team scores. It's more likely that you'll succeed by conceptualizing the result sought, then visualizing a path to achieve it. Course corrections along the way will undoubtedly be required, but monitoring the basic path will provide plenty of notice for those corrections to be made.

EXERCISE: PRODUCE YOUR IMAGINATION

You're on the committee that has asked Joe to come speak to your group. He has accepted. Now you've volunteered to coordinate the logistics for the meeting to plan the event.

The goal is to produce a successful event for Joe and your audience. Take a minute to imagine the event venue and activities that surround hosting it. Make a list of what you'll need and whom you'll need to ensure success.

What I Need	Whom I Need

Glance at the Goal Line

Probably the most overhyped and destructive advice most leadership pundits espouse is to create and focus on goals. Of course, articulating goals is a good thing. In fact, we would be unable to visualize a path to a result if we didn't have a goal in mind from the beginning. However, focusing solely on the goal causes one to miss the mark in several ways.

- **Roadblocks.** First, if our focus is stretched out over the horizon, we're likely to crash into a roadblock along the way. Each day of every organization is replete with challenges that must be overcome or worked around. Some of these issues are significant enough to require the path to be adjusted.

- **Attrition.** Second, goals are ideals. They're not people. Yet it's people working in concert that achieves goals. Forgetting that people are involved at every level of attainment is a dangerous precedent that often results in unnecessary attrition. When good people leave, organizations tend to slip backward. It takes precious time and resources to restore the forward momentum. Avoiding this consequence requires focusing on the immediate a bit more often.

- **Incremental Success.** Third, productivity is about advancing incrementally. To advance incrementally, we must focus on the short-term action plan throughout the day. It's the only way to ensure that advancement is in fact occurring.

The best way to move forward incrementally toward a long-range goal is to *glance at the goal line* but not obsess about it. Harkening back to our quarterback, he must constantly assess how each play will move the ball down the field while also remembering that reaching the goal line is the underlying reason for moving the ball down the field in the first place.

A natural balance can be struck between these two ideas—*visualizing the path* and *glancing at the goal line*—to ensure that our leadership behaviors are effectively focusing our time and efforts and those of our team. Finding that balance begins with being aware of the natural tension between the path and the goal. Adjusting our own focus to reflect the urgency of the day and the urgency of the objectives best communicates to others what is most important right now.

EXERCISE: THE SIMPLEST DESCRIPTION

One method for balancing the importance of the objectives and the maintenance of forward progress is to describe the ultimate goal(s) in the simplest form possible. For example, the goal of a professional speaker's business can be described in three very simple statements:

- Create content.
- Cultivate clients.
- Deliver content.

When mired in the details of a busy workday, our professional speaker can glance up at a sticky note she's pasted on her computer monitor, see these three components to her business, and ask herself, "Is what I'm doing right now advancing me on my path toward one of those three goals?" If so, she can return to her efforts with even more focus and vigor. If not, she can reassess what she should be doing to stay on the path that will help her reach her goal.

Take a moment to think about a current project or business model you have. What are its three or four most fundamental components? Write them down:

- _____

- _____

- _____

Hang this list where you can see it. Glance at it throughout the day to determine if your actions are focused on your goals and that of your organization.

The list produced by the last exercise will align long-term objectives with short-term behaviors. In other words, it provides a point of balance between *visualizing a path* and *glancing at the goal line.*

Call Time-Out

Since we're beating the football analogy to death in this chapter, here's one final connection: when a quarterback gets to the line of scrimmage and sees things that aren't "right" to him, he will try to change the play audibly.

Making audible changes takes time, and the thirty-second clock is always ticking. Sometimes the audible changes take too long to get the ball snapped on time, so instead of taking a delay-of-game penalty, the quarterback will stand up and call a time-out.

The fundamental purpose of the time-out is to regroup, get everyone back onto the same page, and increase the likelihood that the next play will be successful.

In fact, the use of time-outs to regroup is rampant in all sports—and for good reason. A fundamental premise of teamwork is that all team members are working together. When that cohesiveness begins to break down, it's imperative to stop and rebuild it through communication. Without cohesiveness, there is no "team"—it's just a bunch of people running amok.

Funny thing though, the idea of a time-out is rarely used effectively in the business world. Sure, many organizations have regular staff or team meetings. However, the regularly scheduled staff/team meeting misses the point of a time-out. When something is scheduled, it can't be dynamic. Those are two diametrically opposed concepts. The time-out should be both spontaneous and used *only* when regrouping will produce the intended result—team cohesiveness.

We can also use time-outs to insert a short break into the middle of our meeting-after-meeting-after-teleconference days. A brief five-minute time-out allows us to gather together quickly to address critical issues, to yuk it up for a minute and vent some stress, or to simply sit quietly and regenerate. The renewal that can come from a five-minute break is amazing in terms of attitude and energy—the topic of the next chapter.

Developing Field Vision and the Waterfall Effect

Leaders must produce results. It's a fundamental tenet of leadership. A key factor in doing so is developing and exercising field vision. The Waterfall Effect results here when we can visualize the path to the objectives set, remember to glance up at the goal line throughout our hectic days (without obsessing on it), and use time-outs effectively for our teams and for ourselves.

CHAPTER 3

Keeping the Glass Half-Full
The Impact of Attitude on Group Psyche

Naysayers are the cancer in any team or organization. They wield a disproportionate amount of power over the others in the group. Whether their tactics are direct confrontation or background grumbling, those with negative attitudes can throw sludge on the entire effort—resulting in reduced energy, lower productivity, and negatively affected attitudes.

Those in leadership positions must pay particular attention to team members' moods. At its core, performance (and its sibling, productivity) is greatly influenced by the attitude each person brings to the effort. How people feel about themselves, the group, their environment, the project at hand, and the organization all play into how much effort they bring to bear.

Everyone has a disposition, and those dispositions can vary greatly. Some people are naturally upbeat or "happy." Others are more even-keeled, and still, others are generally pessimistic. Though we may have some control over who joins our team, we have little control over the inherent disposition of each member. However, there are several things we can do to increase the likelihood of creating and maintaining a generally positive attitude within the group.

Cultivate Every Relationship

The throwaway line here is this: customer relationship management—it's not just for sales anymore! That means it's incumbent on anyone in a leadership position to develop an individual relationship with each team member. It's not enough to have a good working rapport with the group in general. A leader must have a relationship with each individual in the group in order to understand how each person contributes to the team dynamic.

STORY: THE NETWORKER

Tracie is the director of training for a Seattle-based global organization. She came to her position from a Fortune 500 company. While at her previous job, Tracie developed a number of relationships with her team members, other people in the training department, and throughout the entire organization. Several years after starting her current job, a position opened in a different department that Tracie knew she had the perfect person for. (It was her old boss!) Because they had developed such a good relationship while Tracie was at her previous job, she felt very comfortable contacting her former supervisor to tell her about the job. Today, Tracie and her former boss work at the same company and have the opportunity to further their relationship—all to the benefit of the organization.

The moral of Tracie's story is that because the relationships were strong within the group while Tracie was there, she was able to contact a team member years down the line and be of service again. In fact, the worst thing that can happen to a leader who develops a strong individual relationship with each team member is that a team member may move on out into the world!

Mandate Dignity and Respect

The obvious is often forgotten in the business world. A simple truth worth remembering every single day is that people want to be treated with dignity and respect. This is more *and* less than the proverbial

Golden Rule. Most people simply want to feel like they matter—that they're something more than part of the *human resource*, something more than just a *payroll liability*.

It's easy to see how we lose track of dignity and respect when we couch a discussion in those demeaning and negative terms. The irony is that without those very people, the organization doesn't exist. More importantly, as we move forward into the larger global world where manual and entry-level labor are performed by much-lower-paid individuals, those who can do more will begin to demand more dignity and respect.

Most leaders speak of treating their people with dignity and respect, but how do we test that? How do we, as leaders, ensure that we are actually treating our people that way? The simple answer is to introspectively consider how we really view our people and to look at how we treat them every day.

When we view our people as valuable individuals, treating them with dignity and respect is easy.

EXERCISE: WITH DIGNITY

Here's a great litmus test for how we treat our people. Write down the names of the last three people you had to let go—for any reason, whether performance, downsizing, or something else.

- _____

- _____

- _____

Now go back and place a check mark by the ones whom you would feel comfortable calling up today and asking out to lunch.

Embrace the Risk of Failure

So much is made of succeeding that we forget that we learn more from failure. When we are successful, we *assume* we did all the right things. When we fail, we *analyze* the reasons for it and hope to learn how to avoid repeating the experience. But of course, failure brings with it great risk—like losing our jobs or our money.

This fear of failure is a basic human reaction that is only exacerbated by a never-ending admonishment to succeed that flows through every part of the human experience. Our stock markets depend on it. Our advertising is replete with examples of it. Nonprofits bank on your support to help them succeed. The examples go on and on. Yet the risk of failure is ever present. In essence, failure is always an option—in every endeavor and in every organization—yet we not too secretly cringe at the thought of it.

To triumph over the fear of failure and to keep team members positive and pointed in the right direction, the best course of action is to embrace the risk of that failure and move forward in spite of it. As the old saying goes, "Courage is not the absence of fear, but the ability to overcome it." When a leader demonstrates courage, the team's collective psyche is flooded with positive messaging.

STORY: IN THE FACE OF LONG ODDS

Several years ago, I received a call informing me that my business partner (Tree) had taken a very bad fall while rock climbing. He had crushed both of his heels. The X-rays looked like a hand grenade had blown up in each foot.

Enduring extensive surgery, Tree's heels were "stitched" back together using eleven pins and dozens of screws. The prognosis was not good. Tree

---

would walk again, but he would likely need to use canes for the rest of his life. First though, he had to spend four months in a wheelchair and make sure not to put any weight on his feet whatsoever.

Of course, the doctor didn't know Tree. At his first postoperative appointment, Tree asked the doctor if he could go into a pool. You see, Tree had found a rehabilitation center near his home. They had a lift capable of lifting him from his wheelchair and into the pool, where he could kick his feet back and forth to maintain leg strength. (He'd also had his brother rig up his weight set so he could wheel himself under the machine and use it to maintain his upper-body strength!)

Every day for four months, Tree went to the pool and kicked. He also wheeled himself under his weight machine and did his upper-body exercises several times each day. After four months, it was time for Tree to start learning to walk again. Miraculously, his muscles had atrophied only 20 percent, whereas most patients in a similar situation lose 80 percent of their muscle.

Tree persisted through the rest of his rehabilitation with the same determination all the while facing the fear that he might never regain the freedom of movement he'd had before the accident. It was painful, agonizing at times, to learn to walk again. Progress was slow and often immeasurable, but Tree kept at it doggedly.

Nine months after his fall, Tree approached the rock where he had fallen. Rigged up, he began to make the climb that had evaded him only a few months earlier. After belaying back down, Tree stored away his climbing gear and took up surfing. You see, the sand was a better place for him to walk and exercise the newly formed tendons and ligaments in his heels.

What Tree demonstrated was embracing the risk of failure. The nation's best heel doctor had told him he'd be unlikely to walk without canes. Had he listened, Tree would undoubtedly be hobbling around today on his canes. But Tree decided he would embrace that risk of failure and drive forward the best he could. Today, Tree continues to make a positive mark on everyone who hears his story—lifting them up.

Keeping the Glass Half-Full and the Waterfall Effect

Productivity is about getting things done. People, not organizations, must act to get things done. How our people feel about themselves, the team, and the organization matters greatly when it comes to how well they act. When a leader cultivates every relationship, mandates (and demonstrates) dignity and respect, and embraces the risk of failure, the team will maintain a more positive attitude and produce better results. Better results are a hallmark of the Waterfall Effect.

CHAPTER 4

Leveraging the Value of Silence
The Benefits of Being Quiet

The modern world is a loud, frenetic place. There are constant demands for our attention. Whether it's a new e-mail or text alerts, ringing phones, or coworkers tugging at us, the interruptions and distractions we suffer have a profound effect on our peace of mind and our ability to get things done.

As we mature in our careers, these demands only increase. More responsibility, higher levels of expectation, and a larger pool of people seeking our direction accompany each upward step. Whether it's at work, in the community, or at home, leaders struggle to process all these demands, stay abreast of what's going on, and ensure that forward progress is being made.

One tool every leader can use is silence. Leveraging the value of silence is very powerful. The reason is simple: by being quiet, you encourage those around you to think and communicate with you. Assuming you're working with reasonably capable people who have a basic understanding of their responsibilities, remaining quiet allows you to leverage their abilities to get their work done. Counterintuitively, it also tends to develop a stronger bond between the two of you. That's because when they are actively participating in the process (by thinking and talking), they feel more engaged. Let's explore that a little further.

Engagement Is Something *They* Do

Much is made in leadership and productivity circles of employee engagement. Studies have repeatedly demonstrated that employees who are more engaged with their jobs and their organizations perform at higher levels. Higher levels of performance create better results for everyone—the Waterfall Effect. Therefore, as leaders, we just need our people to be more engaged, right? If only it were that simple.

A fundamental reality about engagement is that it's something *they* do! Leaders cannot mandate engagement—no group e-mail can be sent out dictating that, for example, starting tomorrow, everyone must arrive at work fully engaged. It's an obvious fact, but one most leadership discussions tiptoe around. The reason is that getting people engaged is *hard work*. Moreover, it's something that requires ongoing attention and effort. Otherwise, people will slip out of being engaged, with its attendant reduction in performance and productivity.

One of the quickest ways to facilitate engagement is to shut up. That's right! We're talking about listening. The more we listen to our people and draw them out through questions, the more people engage.

Story: Out to Dinner

Several months ago, I visited my stepbrother and his wife. To set the stage, Richard is considerably older than I am—about thirteen years older. When my mother married his father, I was in grade school, and Richard was in college. Therefore, we've never developed a "normal" sibling relationship. It's always been warm and cordial, but over the distance of time.

On our second evening there, we all went out to dinner. During dinner, I had the pleasure of observing one of the finest listeners I have ever seen. Whether Richard was talking to me—someone he'd known casually for forty years—or his wife of thirty years or my girlfriend—whom he'd just met—he was intently listening to what was being said and asking question after question after question. All of us responded by committing 100 percent to the conversation and thoroughly enjoying the evening. We were engaged!

Leaving the restaurant that evening I felt that I'd been made party to a secret. The secret of how Richard had been so wildly successful in his career ... retiring in his mid-fifties to found a camp for adults with developmental disabilities. He was a world-class listener—using his own silence to get everyone around him engaged.

What is the magic of listening? The simplest explanation is to describe the three levels of listening that we use.

- **Level One.** This is basic listening, the listening that's instinctual. It's listening to things and determining their significance to us. It's completely self-absorbed: How does that sound affect me? Is it friend or foe?

- **Level Two.** This is inquisitive listening. The focus is directed outward, but the level of interest is only at the fact-gathering level. We are seeking to understand something the speaker is saying: Then what happened? After that, what do I do next?

- **Level Three.** This is empathetic listening. This type of listening is directed at the speaker, but instead of just wanting to learn something, we are experiencing what they are describing. We are engaged with them, seeing what they're describing and feeling what they are or were feeling: That must have been exciting! You have certainly struggled to achieve that result.

We spend most of our time at Level One listening. So much is going on around us that we must stay attuned to it to ensure our own safety—physical and mental. The problem, of course, is that it's completely self-absorbed. It's hard for people to engage with us when we are self-absorbed. There's nothing in it for them.

Level Two listening occurs when one person is trying to learn about something from the other. The focus is on the speaker, but the benefits are inuring to the listener. It's quasi-self-absorbed, if you will. Because the communication is really just transmitting data, facts, and information, it's not terribly engaging for the speaker beyond the basic transmission.

Level Three listening is where engagement occurs. When the listener is focused on the speaker and feeding back the energy he or she is receiving, the loop of connection closes. The more feedback that comes back to the speaker, the more engaged the speaker becomes with the listener. The more engaged the speaker becomes, the more connected he or she is to the listener, the team, the project, and the organization.

To be Level Three (empathetic) listeners, we need to put ourselves in the speaker's position and imagine what the speaker must be experiencing and how he or she feels. Delivering feedback that confirms our efforts to do so will naturally align the speaker with us. The speaker becomes more engaged in what's being discussed. This is exactly what Richard was able to do during the dinner conversation described above.

Count to Five!

In the hard-driving modern world, many of us fear not being heard at all. Worse yet, we fear being left behind in the rush. It's a natural tendency to push harder and grow louder in the effort to be seen and heard. That's why restaurants get so loud. As the general din rises, everyone talks more loudly. It's an upward spiral that isn't helped by the hard-surface decorating schemes of most modern eateries. But that's a different diatribe.

One of the consequences of driving hard is that we often run right over the answers in all our noise. We want to fill every gap of silence with our pearls of wisdom. We feel the urgent need to justify or explain our position or our actions. We push and push and push for the answer we want. These behaviors often defeat the very purpose of achieving the objective we seek—to learn from others, to determine what others think, to close the deal we wish to close.

One of the great tactics used by good negotiators is to remain quiet. To say what needs to be said and then stop talking … completely … until a response is made. This is extremely hard to perfect because of our human inclination to push forward. But if we can learn to say what needs to be said, then stop talking and *count to five in our heads,* we will often be surprised by what happens.

EXERCISE: TRADING PLACES

The next time you're dining with a colleague, look at him or her and say, "I'd like to trade places with you." Then *count to five in your head* while looking directly at the person. You'll find the response interesting. Moreover, if you do it with several different people individually, you'll find their answers divergent.

The point of this exercise, and its vague statement, is that you have an anticipated response already formulated in your head based on your own experience and preconceived notions. The reality is that there are numerous potential responses to your statement, and learning what other people think you're saying to them can be fascinating—far more fascinating than merely confirming your own position.

As additional fodder for the Count-to-Five suggestion, try including a few body language principles:

- **Reduce Physical Movement.** This conveys a higher status or more power. Consider the "regal" movements of kings and queens.

- **Open Palms Facing Upward.** This conveys an open perspective. It asks for someone to expand on what's being discussed. It seeks their input.

- **Neutral Position.** Remaining physically neutral and upright, as opposed to leaning in (secrecy) or leaning out (superiority), conveys a bargaining position as equals.

The underlying point is that allowing other people to fill in the gaps and communicate their thoughts may produce far better results for us as leaders than driving our own opinions and conclusions into others all the time.

Take "Me" Time

Recent MRI studies confirm what we've long known anecdotally—humans work best in short bursts, not in marathon efforts. To state it more directly, we can remain very focused for relatively short periods of time (about ninety minutes), but then we need a mental break to regenerate and refresh our energy. Attempts at working long hours demonstrate a marked loss of productivity as we move further and further beyond that ninety-minute period. Doubters need only recall their last all-nighter to remember how inefficient the effort was both during and after the fact.

As an aside, it's interesting to note that our sleep cycles run in ninety-minute cycles too. We enter REM sleep—considered a necessary refreshment period—about every ninety minutes. Coincidence? Probably not.

To maximize our effectiveness throughout the day, leaders must take "me" time periodically. It doesn't have to be much. Just five minutes can have a huge impact on how refreshed we are as we enter the next meeting or period of focused effort. A catnap, no matter how short, is an excellent way to clear out the cobwebs and recharge before the next power lunch!

EXAMPLE: THAT "AHA!" MOMENT

Other MRI findings on how the brain works are equally intriguing. One study was seeking to understand how "aha!" moments happen. How do epiphanies occur?

Though still being confirmed, what scientists now believe is that epiphanies occur when "weak signal" ideas are allowed to join in the brain. The problem is that the "working brain"—that part of the brain we use to focus on things—produces a lot of noise, effectively drowning out the weak signal ideas.

> Consequently, it's only when our working brains are quiet that the connections can occur.
>
> That's why we have those "aha!" moments when we're gardening or drifting off to sleep or standing in the shower. Our working brains have quieted down enough to let those disparate ideas find each other.

In the end, the more energized we feel and the better we can focus during our bursts of effort, the more effective and productive we will be. The ancillary benefit is that we won't suffer as much exhaustion and burnout, which is a good thing too.

Leveraging the Value of Silence and the Waterfall Effect

In the modern cacophony of interruptions and distractions, it seems counterintuitive that silence can be such a powerful leadership tool. Yet once explained, the benefits of remaining quiet are obvious. Allowing our team members to be engaged clearly results in higher performance, better productivity, and longer retention. Counting to five after making a statement lets us discover what the listener thinks. It may or may not be what we think, but that knowledge can be powerful nonetheless. Finally, adjusting our work habits to align with our natural rhythms—ninety-minute cycles—produces an environment of increased performance and reduced burnout. Silence is indeed golden.

CHAPTER 5

Peeling Back the Onion
The Reward of Uncovering the
Hidden Potential in Others

I t's a pleasant surprise—that's a leader's experience when someone on the team rises above the fray, especially when it's in an unexpected way.

It happens when we least expect it, and it often comes from someone we didn't know was capable of it. These moments shine over the entire group and the organization. They become part of the organization's lore, legends retold for years in the future. It's a rare and special thing when someone's hidden potential emerges and produces the Waterfall Effect.

But what if we could seek out those abilities? How can we increase the likelihood that people will rise above the expectations we have of them? Is there a way we can uncover the hidden potential in our team members?

The answer is yes, we can uncover that potential. It takes a bit of rejiggering how we see our "human resources" and a bit of patience and open-mindedness, but it's very possible. Making superstars out of our people is a matter of supporting their often-unspoken desire to succeed in ways that interest them. To accomplish this, we need to start at the beginning—at the point of employment.

Every organization hires people to fill a human resource need. The process is relatively straightforward. We post an open position in some public manner, describing the job's duties and responsibilities.

We accept applications from people interested in securing the job. We move through the review and interview process, generally deciding on the right match between candidate and opening. The job is offered to that candidate. The candidate accepts the position and begins his or her employment with the organization.

Throughout the employee's tenure with the organization, the person's performance is measured against the stated duties and responsibilities. The employee advances—in title and salary—if he or she is performing well against those benchmarks.

The above description is perfectly normal and works pretty well. There's one giant problem with it. Because the entire framework is built around a specific job's duties and responsibilities, nothing about the employee's other talents/abilities/interests are taken into consideration. At best, we get what we asked for and rarely more.

Of course, the organization needs to get what it asked for in an employee. Leaders must ensure that result. However, why can't we seek more than that? Why can't we find ways for our people to perform at levels and in ways that are higher than their positions' mere duties and responsibilities? We can, and here are some suggestions on how to make that happen.

Mentoring Redux

In the employment context, mentoring is generally perceived as more experienced people providing guidance and advice to less experienced people *on their career path*. Most of the focus is on how less experienced people can successfully move along their career path. Again, this isn't inherently bad; and in many cases, it's extremely helpful, *assuming the career path is correct or even enough*.

Stepping away from mentoring for a moment and looking at the broader subject of lifestyle and occupation, much is made today of pursuing one's passion and doing what we love. Digging into that discussion further, rarely is pursuing that passion related to our present employment or lifestyle. Most often, we must abandon our current path and find a "better" one. The result, we are assured, will be greater success and happiness.

It's the assertion that a direction change is required that is most misplaced. It's highly disruptive to all involved and can be very risky. What if our organizations and the leaders within those organizations looked at the human resource with more flexibility than all the other resources it has at its disposal? What if mentoring sought to uncover an employee's hidden qualities, interests, and abilities and then aligned those talents with its goals and objectives?

STORY: TAPPING INTO TALENT

Alison ran the operations for a consulting department within a software company. She had thirty-five people in her department, and the company's client base consisted primarily of Fortune 500 companies. Consequently, Alison's focus ranged across the globe and all of its time zones. Managing the logistics of getting work in the door and consultants to do the work was more than a full-time job, not to mention getting the invoices and expenses submitted and paid.

To help her stay on top of everything, Alison hired an administrative assistant—Marybeth—to assist her. Marybeth was a starving artist. She wanted to paint pictures and have gallery openings to attend. The last thing she wanted to do was track expense receipts and file paperwork. Unfortunately for her, the term *starving artist* was apt, and she needed to pay the bills. Fortunately for Alison, Marybeth was very reliable and detail-oriented!

Some months after Marybeth began her job, Alison decided the department needed an operations manual. It was to be a road map everyone in the department could follow when working with new and existing clients on new and existing engagements. Having learned of Marybeth's artistic inclinations during passing conversations with her, Alison assigned the task of creating the operations manual to her.

Marybeth's first question was, "What does one look like, and what does it need to include?" Alison told her she didn't know but suggested that Marybeth start with that question, conduct some research, and get back to her in a few days with some thoughts. This became their process. Marybeth would investigate various aspects of operations manuals, she and Alison would meet to discuss her findings, and any new questions they raised would send Marybeth back into research mode.

About three months later, Marybeth proudly presented Alison with the first copy of the operations manual. It was a thing of beauty. Everything a team member could need was right there—well organized and fully explained. Alison had taken Marybeth's creative abilities and applied it to a departmental need, which resulted in a "win" for Marybeth and for the consulting group.

Marybeth's story may seem inconsequential, even trite, but the epilogue is that when Alison left the group for a new company, Marybeth was promoted to director of operations. Her creative inclinations had been leveraged, and she had found an unlikely path to career and life success.

Here are some specific actions we can take to increase the number of stories like Marybeth's:

- **Making Time.** Carving out time—even scheduling it—to meet and talk with individuals in the group is vitally important to learning what other talents and interests they have. Preferably, this is done away from the structured environment of the office to reduce the weight of the employment relationship.

- **Engaged Listening.** Review the discussion in the last chapter about empathetic listening. The purpose of these conversations is discovery and exploration. We want to learn more about each person, and engaging in Level Three listening helps this effort along.

- **Ferret Out Latent Abilities.** We must pay attention to the conversation to uncover what is not readily apparent. The time spent with our team members should diverge from work and the "job" wherever possible to learn more about what they might bring to the table. The example of using Marybeth's creative talents to produce an operations manual is obvious only after the fact.

Meeting with each person periodically and remaining interested in their interests will pay huge dividends for everyone down the line when we are able to match what they enjoy with what we need done.

Hire Yourself Out of a Job

As noted above, Marybeth was promoted into Alison's position when she left. That advancement was an unintended benefit resulting from Alison's creative mentoring and Marybeth's hard work and positive attitude.

Recreating that success is not as hard as it seems. The trick, again, is to look at the hiring process as an opportunity—an opportunity to find great people, not just people to fill a role. We must always find people with the skills and talents needed to fulfill the needs of the open position, but it's easy to go beyond that baseline and filter for potential too.

Of course, we can't promise more than what the available position offers, but we can seek more in the hiring process. For example, during the interview or onboarding process, why not try out some irregular interview tactics? Here are two that have proven to be very effective:

- **Word Association.** After a candidate has made the internal interview rounds and you are conducting that last meeting with them, ask them to indulge in a word association game with you. Ask them to respond with the first word that comes to mind after you speak a word. If the person is being interviewed for an executive role, use the names of the departments for which they will be responsible. If it's a managerial role, use the names of the people who interviewed them. If it's a line position, use the supervisors' names.

  The point is to gauge several things. First, did they interview the other people or merely respond to the questions being asked? Second, did they form clear pictures and opinions during the process? Third, how do their opinions match the organization's or yours?

- **Office Arrangement.** If the candidate is being interviewed in an office, another useful interview tactic is to ask them how they would arrange the furniture if it was their office.

  This question also gauges several things. First, how do they respond to the unexpected? Second, can they think on their feet? Third, do they have any good ideas? Finally, are they willing to say something different from "It looks fine to me"?

By using the interview process as a way to vet prospective employees for more than just the position available, we can build a stable of talent that we can groom to perform in superstar ways.

> ### EXERCISE: THE PICK OF THE LITTER
>
> Spend a minute thinking about the people in your organization. Using the space below, list three of them whom you *know* could be doing more than they currently are.
>
> • _____
>
> • _____
>
> • _____
>
> **Homework:** Decide what you are going to do about it.

Guide versus Direct

It's often very expedient to simply answer all the questions hurled at us all day long. A quick answer and that person is out of our view-finder. Who cares that we might be answering the same question over and over and over for the same person? Right now, we just need to power through the list of things that need doing.

The problem here is that if we answer every question asked of us, we are training our people to ask us questions. We hired them to solve problems, but the frenetic work environment doesn't allow them enough time to do that effectively. Instead, it seems more expeditious for them to just ask us every question that pops up.

That's just backward. What we need to do is focus on helping our people learn to solve the problems that invariably creep up every day. We can do that by guiding them more and directing them less.

EXAMPLE: WHAT A DRIVER LEARNS

Most of us have driven a car. All of us have ridden in a car. Who do you think learns the route to a new destination better—the driver of the car or the passenger?

The driver does, of course. The reason is that the driver has to pay attention and stay focused on the objective—reaching the destination. The passenger is free to look around and enjoy the ride.

Thus, we need to create more drivers in our organization and fewer passengers.

Creating drivers requires that we put aside what's most expeditious—answering the question (directing)—and carve out some time to elicit an answer (guiding). Call it the Kinder, Gentler Socratic Method. Instead of answering every question being asked of us, start asking questions in response. Here are some that work well:

- What are our options?

- What have we done before?

- What do you think we should do?

Note that the point of these inquiries is *not* to make our people feel inadequate or stupid. The point is to *guide* them to the right answers—to create drivers of solutions. This is not hide-and-seek. It's "let me show you the way." Interestingly, after only a short while, most team members start showing up with a host of options already prepared. In that event, the conversation becomes about which option is best—just another (higher-value) opportunity to ask more questions!

Peeling Back the Onion and the Waterfall Effect

The Waterfall Effect that results when people perform beyond expectation is self-evident. The point of this chapter is to find ways to increase the likelihood of that happening. By revisiting the purpose and method for mentoring our people, we can learn of talents and abilities that go far beyond a job description or career path. Using some innovative tactics during the hiring process, we can gain a glimpse into a candidate's potential to do more than what is posted in the job description. Finally, if we can train ourselves to guide our people versus direct them, we gain greater efficiency and effectiveness.

CHAPTER 6

Setting the Bar
The Importance of Establishing
and Maintaining Proper Expectations

Disappointment. Frustration. Angst. Anger. These are the feelings we experience when our expectations aren't met. They are very powerful feelings and can drive significant changes in behavior. For instance, few people will return to an expensive restaurant if the food or service doesn't meet their expectations. The same can be said for business relationships. If we hire a firm to do a job and they don't deliver a high-quality product within a reasonable time frame, we generally look for a new firm the next time we need that service.

STORY: THE WINNER DINNER

Recently, friends went to a new restaurant that was getting great buzz. It was a small place that didn't take reservations. They went on a Friday night around eight o'clock. Walking into the restaurant, they could see that it was busy. All the tables were taken, and several groups were waiting to be seated. They grabbed a menu to review and looked it over. A moment later, the hostess approached and informed them (pleasantly) that the restaurant would love to have their business, but it would be at least forty-five minutes before they'd be seated. Considering the relatively late hour, the couple left the restaurant and went elsewhere.

> Here's the twist: the couple raved about the great service! They were very appreciative that the hostess was both forthcoming and nice when she told them how long the wait was going to be. Not only did they tell everyone they'd be returning; but some weeks later, they did return. The restaurant had earned zealous customers long before the couple ever spent a dime!

Suffice it to say that a fundamental tenet of success for every organization is to establish and maintain proper expectations. This is true both internally and externally. That is, good expectation management needs to occur among the people inside the organization and between the organization's people and those with whom the organization interacts in the outside world. Interestingly though, people and organizations fail to properly manage expectations all the time.

Expectation management is a double-edged sword. It's easy to meet or exceed an expectation that's been properly set and managed. That's one for the "win" column. However, it's just as easy to get a check mark in the "lose" column when an expectation isn't properly set or managed.

Fundamentally, expectation management is about communication— establishing and maintaining good expectations happen through good communication. Moreover, this is an area where leaders must serve on the front lines—by demonstrating through our actions the proper way to set expectations and the proper way to maintain them. This is true regardless of whether we're dealing with people inside the organization or with people on the outside.

Start on the Right Foot

The very best time to set expectations is when a relationship is new. This goes for new employees as well as new customers/clients. There is a blank slate at that moment, and everything is open for discussion. Of course, there is some base expectation about how this relationship will proceed—a standard-in-the-industry sort of thing. However, this particular relationship has yet to get under way, so why not take this opportunity to clearly articulate some basic ground rules such as these:

- How and how often communication will occur

- When and how work product will be delivered

- The protocol for escalation of issues

- How invoicing or payroll occurs and when payments are expected

This list may appear obvious, but it covers the basics of every working relationship. Instead of assuming the details of these relationship cornerstones, a brief conversation covering the details of this list is in everyone's best interest.

EXAMPLE: LEAD FROM THE BEGINNING

An attorney friend schedules an "intake appointment" with every new client he receives. The purpose of the appointment is to discuss the ground rules for the relationship. On his list of things to cover are (1) that he generally checks his e-mail about once per hour and will usually respond within twenty-four hours and (2) that if a client needs him to see something sooner than that, the client needs to call him directly or call his assistant to communicate that urgency.

Many people recoil in horror at the thought of having this conversation with clients and customers. They feel speaking with a new client in this manner is the antithesis of good service. However, before rejecting this process out of hand, understand that this lawyer is a partner in a very large law firm with a very successful practice. One of the tools he uses to maintain that success is to have direct and clear conversations with every new client about what they both expect during their relationship.

Setting good expectations is the first step toward developing strong and productive relationships. Leaders are well advised to consider an "intake" conversation with new team members as well as new customers/clients. The very worst that can happen is that a great conversation about how to work well together takes place.

Clarity Is King

If establishing and maintaining expectations is essentially about communication, then good communication is necessary to be successful. As obvious as this is, it's amazing how bad most of us are at clearly communicating our expectations.

EXERCISE: THE ASAP CONUNDRUM

Grab a pencil or pen and please use the space below to write down *when* ASAP is:

_____

That's right. ASAP doesn't exist. It's meant to convey urgency, but it lacks any shred of clarity. Its siblings—Top Priority, Urgent, Now—have similar failings. For example, if our assistant is leaving on vacation in an hour and we just handed him the fifth ASAP of the day, it's likely he is thinking that means a week from now when he gets back from vacation. That's probably not what we were thinking ...

Using terms such as ASAP is lazy deadline setting. It's a leader's job to set deadlines that are clear and specific. It is not a subordinate's job to wade through the stack of vague deadlines and intuit which one is *the* most urgent, which one is second most urgent, and so on.

Setting good expectations requires specificity. We must use an actual date whenever we give work to others. The same is true when we are communicating to our clients/customers about the work we're doing for them. The flip side of this coin, which is discussed in detail in the next chapter, is to extract specific dates from others when vague deadlines are being offered.

EXAMPLE: TO THE BOTTOM IT GOES

After delivering a time management seminar, I was talking with a senior staff manager and a couple of executives. The topic turned to the ASAP diatribe I often launch into during a conversation about expectation management. The senior staff manager said, right in front of the executives, that any work that comes into her department with an ASAP deadline affixed to it gets placed at the bottom of the pile—below all the other work with specific deadlines on it. The reason? That's *As Soon As Possible.*

~ 43 ~

Good leadership is about clarity. Fortunately, so is good expectation management. Getting a specific date affixed to work assignments goes a long way toward achieving both.

Be a Hero, Not a Zero

Humans are optimists. It's part of the glue that keeps us communal and able to work together through thick and thin. Optimism is part of the entrepreneurial drive and the ability (and the desire) to seek what's beyond the horizon.

Optimism also gets us into trouble. We tend to think tasks will take less time than they actually take. We tend to overcommit our time and agree to get everything done "right away" or "by day's end." The unfortunate result is that we get behind on our deadlines, we disappoint those with whom we work, and we feel overwhelmed and stressed out.

Essentially, our optimistic tendencies drive poor expectation setting—for us and for others. Effective leaders understand this tendency and adjust to it. The results are much better when a project is delivered on its due date instead of a day late.

EXAMPLE: MAKING DELIVERIES COUNT

Outdoorplay is an online retailer of outdoor gear such as tents, sleeping bags, and camp stoves. (See www.outdoorplay.com for more information.) Customers who choose the free ground shipping option are told that their order will be delivered in five to seven business days. It doesn't matter if the customer submits the order online or over the phone or if the customer is in nearby Portland, Oregon, or across the country in Miami, Florida: they are told to *expect* their order in five to seven business days.

Why is this? It's clear that a ground shipment traveling less than one hundred miles will take less time to arrive than one traveling three thousand miles. The reason is simple: UPS (Outdoorplay's shipping company) virtually guarantees that all ground shipments in the continental United States will be delivered within five to seven business days. Given that fact, Outdoorplay has decided to proactively set the proper expectations with the customer. As a result, 99 percent of the time, Outdoorplay meets or exceeds the expectations it has set for its customers. Consequently, the company has a repeat/referral percentage (i.e., the percentage of customers who are repeat customers or referred by others) that is the envy of the industry.

Being a hero and not a zero is simple. Set the expectation at the outset based on a realistic time frame for its completion. Being even an hour late can produce devastating results—in the form of disappointment—so there's really nothing to lose by pushing deadlines out as far as reasonably possible.

Here are some hints on how to do this:

- **Never Today.** Never commit to getting anything done today. Most of us have a full plate today, and all of those things were commitments we'd already made! If we are met with resistance on "tomorrow," ask what's driving the deadline. If it's truly an emergency (and some are), see what other things can be bumped to make room for this one. (Note: After meeting this urgent deadline, circle back with the other person and discuss how to avoid this in the future—just more expectation management!)

- **Regularly Review Commitments.** Forgetting what's already on our plate is a trap for the unwary. Knowing how much needs to be done today, tomorrow, and so on helps us work with deadlines more efficiently and accurately. Develop a mechanism to capture all that needs doing—a.k.a., a to-do list—and regularly review it throughout the day to minimize the risk of overcommitting. (Adding a queuing mechanism to the to-do list makes the list dynamic and greatly enhances our ability to see what needs doing when. QuietSpacing® is one such way to do that. End of shameless self-promotion.)

- **Overcommunicate Changes.** True emergencies invariably arise. They act like explosions in our best laid plans. When an urgent matter forces us to clear the decks, it's incumbent on us to communicate the changes to the recipients of the work being bumped. Send an e-mail or make a phone call explaining the situation and when "their" project can now be anticipated. It's not perfect, but it's part of the reality of managing expectations in the modern world.

Setting the Bar and the Waterfall Effect

Just like a waterfall starts by water flowing over the top of a cliff, setting and managing expectations is a preliminary element in producing a series of benefits that cascade down through the organization and out into the customer/client base. The urgency we all feel in the modern work world needs to be tempered when we're working with others. By starting on the right foot, the relationships we develop will be based on a mutually understood method of working together. Making sure that our communications with each other are clear and specific will ensure the setting of proper expectations. Finally, harnessing our optimism increases the likelihood that we'll be heroes and not zeros.

CHAPTER 7

Triaging Priorities
The Reality of Constant Appraisal
of What Needs Doing "Now"

The modern work environment is not unlike the hospital emergency room—that is, there is a constant flow of people demanding attention. At its core, triage—the process used by emergency rooms to determine who needs medical care most urgently—is fundamentally a workflow method.

As its name implies, people in an emergency room need care urgently. The severity of injuries present can vary at any moment, which requires medical personnel to engage in a constant triaging process. In other words, the decision of who gets treatment when is not static. It can change in the blink of an eye. A ten-car pileup on the freeway can result in a long wait for a patient complaining of nausea who was next in line just moments ago.

The same is true of the modern work world. Technology has made it possible for us to send and receive requests for information, products, time, and materials at near-light speeds. As a result, we do just that. We send (and receive) those requests minute by minute, hour by hour, and day by day. This is both good and bad.

The good part is the speed of information exchange and all its resulting benefits vastly increase. The bad part is that we feel overwhelmed by the number of requests for our attention. In addition, our productivity and the productivity of our team members suffer. Moreover, we tend to respond to requests based on the status of the person who sends them and on vague deadlines (such as "ASAP") instead of on which request is the most important in terms of our goals and the goals of the organization.

Example: Clara Barton's Early Years

Many associate Clara Barton with the founding of the American Red Cross, which is accurate. Most don't know that Clara Barton was a pioneer in medical science.

During the Civil War, a group of injured Union soldiers made their way to Baltimore, Maryland, where Clara lived. She took them to her sister's house, where she separated the soldiers by the severity of their injuries. This was a revolutionary concept. Previously, order of care was determined by such factors as rank, wait time, and race.

The French in World War I later called Clara's system triage, but the concept was first applied many years earlier to save the lives of as many Union troops as Clara could.

Leaders in today's frantic work environments are constantly engaging in a similar process. They aren't making life-and-death decisions, but the process of determining which tasks or requests for attention are most important and which ones can wait is essentially triaging. The triage decisions are also dynamic since new demands for attention and work product are constantly being made.

Staying responsive, effective, and productive under these circumstances requires leaders to develop good triaging skills. The following suggestions will help.

Realize That Multitasking Is Impossible

In early 2010, Stanford University released a study that concluded in part that people just don't multitask very well. But we don't even need to look to science to know this is true. Just ask yourself whether you've ever been in someone else's office trying to have a conversation with them while they checked their e-mail. How productive was the experience? Not very, right?

The reason we don't multitask well is founded more on an economic theory called a *switch cost* than anything else. A switch cost is the "cost" (in this case, time) of switching between processes. That's because every time you switch between things—one task to another—it takes a moment to come up to speed on the new task before you can be productive. Thus, as you can see, the more switches that occur, the higher the cost in lost time.

EXERCISE: SO YA THINK YOU'RE DIFFERENT?

Many people take objection to the position that multitasking is impossible. The following exercise will dissuade you of this feeling. It's an exercise borrowed (with changes) from Dave Crenshaw's book *The Myth of Multitasking*.

- Find something you can time yourself with, or ask someone to time you.

- Get a blank piece of paper and a pen or pencil.

- At the top of the paper, write the word *project*, which is seven letters long.

- Underneath, create two lines of seven dashes each, like this:

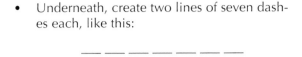

- Start the timer. For the first exercise, write the first letter of *project*—a *p*—on the top line, and then write the number *1* on the bottom line. Return to the top line to write an *r* next to the *p,* and then back down to write a *2* next to the *1*. Stop the timer when you've spelled *project* out completely on the top line and written the numbers *1* through *7* on the bottom line.

- Once you've made a note of how much time it took you to do this part of the exercise, go ahead and set the paper up again the same way. Start the timer again.

- This time we're going to change one rule. You're going to spell out the word *project* fully across the top line before moving to the bottom line to count out the numbers *1* through *7*.

- Stop the timer when you've completed these individual tasks.

The result is that the first exercise should take you about 65 percent longer to complete because you are alternating between spelling and counting with each action you take. In the second exercise, your brain focuses entirely on spelling until you're finished, and then moves down to counting. As a result, you incur no switch costs along the way.

The point here is that trying to triage workloads in a nonsystematic manner is just another form of multitasking. It's inefficient. Instead, stop periodically throughout the day—as often as necessary—and intentionally focus your attention on the triaging process. It's an administrative task by definition, but it's a necessary one that needs to be done well. Moreover, when leaders triage well, the projects and people they lead are more effective and efficient too.

Develop a Simple Sorting System

A precept to effective triage is a system of categorization into which each request and demand can be placed. Like the medical form of triage, we need a way to assess what each request constitutes before we can compare it against other existing demands. Numerous time management systems espouse their own method for parsing inbound requests. Whether it's David Allen's *Getting Things Done*, the FranklinCovey system, or another method, the point here is that we need one that works quickly and simply.

Categorizing each item allows us to separate the important from the less important. By decluttering the landscape and gaining a clearer view of what's at hand, the ability to get back to work (on the right things) is rapidly advanced.

It will come as no surprise that the author recommends the QuietSpacing® method for categorizing each request/demand before aligning (and realigning) our priorities. The QuietSpacing® method divides all inbound items into one of four categories:

- **Trash.** This group of items is made up of those things we simply don't need anymore. They can be thrown away or deleted. (Note that many, many, many of the things sitting in our physical and electronic workspaces are Trash. We just need to muster the courage to toss them!)

- **Archive.** These are items that you may someday need to retrieve for some future purpose. Until then though, they can go far, far away—like into an off-site storage or archival hard drives or the document management system.

- **Reference.** Like Archive items, Reference items are those things we may need in the future. But in this case, we use them to conduct our day-to-day activities. Therefore, they need to be *stored* near-far away.

- **Work.** Ah, now we're getting down to it. Work is everything that needs to get done—by us or by others. This is the stuff we've been searching for, but it's been buried under all the Trash, Archive, and Reference items.

If you find yourself unable to categorize a particular item into one of the four categories above, ask this simple question: Does something further need to be done with this? If the answer is no, it must *necessarily* be Trash, Archive, or Reference (which are all what we call Closed items). If the answer is yes, it can *only* be Work (which is the only Open category).

EXERCISE: A SIMPLE TRIAGE

Turn to your e-mail inbox. Open up the e-mail at the top of the list. Is it Trash, Archive, Reference, or Work? If it's Trash, delete it. If it's Archive or Reference, create a file (if necessary) and file it away. If it's Work, move down to the next e-mail. Repeat this process for the next nine messages in your inbox.

You will find that using a quick and simple sorting method helps you clear out the "white noise" of Closed items, allowing you to focus your attention on what needs to be done now.

Though this book lacks room to delve further into the QuietSpacing® method, its high-level architecture serves our purpose here. We have just started the process of effective triage by accurately (and simply) separating all of our inbound demands so we can see what really needs our attention.

Secure Clear Deadlines

This is a sibling suggestion to the Clarity Is King suggestion made in the last chapter. Securing clear deadlines for work is mandatory for effective triaging. Stating the obvious, we can't determine which task is most important when all of them are due ASAP. We need finer granularity. We need dates. Without this level of specificity, the triaging effort is just a guessing game.

Needing specific deadlines is obvious, but getting them can be difficult. This is where true leadership enters the picture. It is incumbent on us to secure these specified deadlines by whatever manner is necessary. The effort may require diplomacy, or it may require directness. Either way, we must ensure that it happens. Without this information, we cannot perform at our highest level and neither can our teams.

In the end, it's just a negotiation. We're negotiating away from vagueness (ASAP) toward specificity (e.g., Tuesday next week). If we approach it as a negotiation, it's easy to see how to achieve our goal in a manner that maintains relationship harmony and produces better results because we can properly order the demands for our attention.

Triaging Priorities and the Waterfall Effect

A cornerstone to good leadership is getting things done. In the frenetic modern work world, leaders must constantly triage all the demands coming at them and at their team members to ensure their limited resources are focused on the right projects at the right time.

By deliberately focusing on the triaging process and using a good sorting system that mandates clear deadlines, we can regularly produce the Waterfall Effect for our team, our organization, and our clients/customers.

CHAPTER 8

Cascading Benefits

This discussion started by asking what the most important asset of an organization is. The answer was *time*. That's because everything an organization does occurs within the context of time. The organization executes its mission over the course of time, and because time is nonrenewable, how the organization leverages time is of utmost importance.

We next addressed the question of whose time is most important within the organization. The answer was that *your* time is the most important. The reasoning eschews organizational structure and focuses on the simple fact that organizations are made up of people. Therefore, what each person does is either valuable or not valuable to the organization and promotes or doesn't promote a sense of success in the individual. Because success is a feeling and not a result for people, the true objective is to marry the individual's sense of success with the organization's objectives. Finally, we established that leadership is about action and not title or words. This means that the individual contribution is of fundamental importance to the organization's overall success.

That analysis brought us to the "why" question. Why does any of this really matter? The answer was because of the Waterfall Effect. The Waterfall Effect is the cascade of benefits that occurs when the right people (leaders) are focused on the right activities and working with the right people. It flows down through the organization and out into the customer/client base.

Once our foundation was in place, we spent the rest of our time looking at how to produce the Waterfall Effect. We determined that six principles facilitate our ability to reproduce the Waterfall Effect over time:

- Developing Field Vision
- Keeping the Glass Half-Full
- Leveraging the Value of Silence
- Peeling Back the Onion
- Setting the Bar
- Triaging Priorities

Through explanation, example, story, and exercise, eighteen suggestions were described that instructed us on how to reproduce the Waterfall Effect at every level in every organization. The only remaining question to answer is,

How Will You Produce Your Next Waterfall Effect?